MAKING SENSE OF BEHAVIOUR

EXERCISING SELF-CONTROL

by

Rob Long

A NASEN PUBLICATION

Published in 1999

ISBN 1 901485 08 0

Published by NASEN.
NASEN is a company limited by guarantee, registered in England and Wales. Company No. 2674379.
NASEN is a registered charity. Charity No. 1007023.

Further copies of this book and details of NASEN's many other publications may be obtained from the Publications Department at its registered office: NASEN House, 4/5 Amber Business Village, Amber Close, Amington, Tamworth, Staffs. B77 4RP.
Tel: 01827 311500; Fax: 01827 313005
Email: welcome@nasen.org.uk; Website: www.nasen.org.uk

Cover design by Raphael Creative Design.
Typeset in Times by J. C. Typesetting and printed in the United Kingdom by Stowes (Stoke-on-Trent).

Contents

Preface

Exercising Self-control is one of eight booklets in the series *Making Sense of Behaviour* by Rob Long. The others are *Understanding and Supporting Depressed Children and Young People; Developing Self-esteem through Positive Entrapment for Pupils facing Emotional and Behavioural Difficulties; Friendships; Not Me, Miss! The Truth about Children who Lie; Challenging Confrontation: Information and Techniques for School Staff; Supporting Pupils with Emotional and Behavioural Difficulties through Consistency;* and *Learning to Wave: Some Everyday Guidelines for Stress Management.*

The first five titles give practical ideas and information for teachers to use with children with worrying behaviours in their classes. These are written to help teachers both understand and change some of the difficulties that children might experience (depression, lack of self-control, low self-esteem, friendship problems and lying).

Challenging Confrontation gives information and techniques for teachers to use when dealing with argumentative, angry and difficult pupils. *Supporting Pupils with Emotional and Behavioural Difficulties through Consistency* advocates a whole-school approach for low-level misbehaviours whilst *Learning to Wave* is written for teachers themselves. It contains advice about coping with the stress which might arise from dealing with children with behavioural problems.

Each book stands alone but when read as a set the behavioural issues and their solutions overlap and this emphasises the need for positive and consistent strategies to be put into place throughout the school.

Acknowledgements
The author and publishers wish to express their grateful thanks to Lorna Johnston, Agnes Donnelly and Dorothy Smith for their helpful suggestions and comments.

Exercising Self-Control

Introduction

There are many children, of all ages, who are described by school staff as being impulsive and lacking self-control. These children respond to sudden urges without consideration of timing or the consequences of their behaviour. They seem to convert ideas into immediate action, "bypassing" thought. In many cultures impulsive behaviour is viewed as undesirable behaviour and modified through socialisation at home and school.

It is worth stressing that self-control is one of the skills that is missing in those children who have quick, explosive tempers. These are the children who have a low tolerance of frustration and will quickly hit out impulsively as a way of releasing their anger. While improving their self-control is not the only way of helping them to take control of their anger, it can play an important part.

One of the means by which self-control is achieved is through the child developing "inner speech". This process has three phases:

1. The child's behaviour is controlled, directed and modelled by adults.
   "Let's tidy everything up before we have our drink."
2. The child's own covert speech of what the adult has told them in similar situations.
   "I put toys away so that we know where they are next time we want them."
3. Finally the child's own covert speech controls his/her behaviour through inner speech.

Self-control is achieved through children using language to think about their own behaviour. Thinking or cognition refers to a set of related processes including:

- perceiving
- problem solving
- recalling information
- processing information

Thinking involves not only what we think about, the products of thinking, for example, "where am I going tomorrow?", but also how we think - the very process by which we remember things, the coding of information electrochemically in the brain.

In the real world this process can best be seen when an adult works to improve the self-control of a child who finds it difficult to concentrate and complete any one task. We will consider this approach later as a useful strategy for infant-aged children who lack self-control.

Why do some children lack self-control?
Like most behaviours there is rarely one simple explanation. Poor self-control can be a symptom of:

- attention deficit disorder
- neurological damage
- drug abuse
- learning difficulties
- parenting style
- acute anxiety

In some children several of these may be causing the lack of self-control.

Remember if you are ever concerned about a child's difficulties then refer to specialists who can provide you with further advice and assessment.

In school a lack of self-control results in difficulties in a number of areas. Learning can be affected because these children find it harder to concentrate and to ignore distractions. Relationships with adults can/may become negative as the impulsive behaviour can cause disruptions in lessons and peers can find such behaviour unpredictable, threatening and worrying. The end result can be that such children are rejected and become isolated. There can be a real danger of their behaviour worsening and then being excluded from activities, class or school.

Indications of poor self-control
- Gives in easily to temptation.
- Quickly "wound up" by other children.
- Low toleration of frustration.
- Rushes to do a task before all instructions are given.
- Say they will do one thing, but then do another.

Why "exercising" self-control?

The title may seem inappropriate to those who believe self-control to be something that children either have or haven't got. If this is the case there is little we can do to help such children. But if we see self-control as comprising a range of specific skills, then we can design programmes that we know will develop those skills. Children can then work with specific activities that will enhance their skills and contribute overall to an increase in self-control. Just as when one is ill in bed for a time and one's muscles weaken, one knows that very small periods of exercise will gradually increase one's strength, so too can self-control be developed, increased and strengthened.

Self-control and its components

Children with self-control can:

- Know how much control they have over situations.
- Define a problem, produce and evaluate options and make a choice.
- Think before acting - through inner speech.
- Accurately assess their skills in different situations.
- Use their imagination as a means of evaluating usefulness of a plan.
- Imagine different perspectives in situations.
- Understand how their behaviour can lead to positive or negative outcomes.
- Use their memory to appreciate different lengths of time.

Developing inner speech control

Because "inner speech control" is so important to the development of self-control it is worth elaborating it separately, though there will be further ideas to develop it later.

If we are concerned about an infant-aged child then we can utilise the following model as a strategy to increase the likelihood of a child acquiring it.

Step 1 - Adult as model

The adult carries out the task and provides a "running commentary" of what they are doing. "Now let me see, I think I'll colour that part blue. I must go slowly around that line or I'll go over it." The adult is showing the child the instructions and decisions that they are having to make at each step.

Step 2 - Adult as commentator
The child is now encouraged to do the same task while the adult talks them through, monitoring their behaviour. "Yes that's good, you'll need to go slowly around the face." The adult may even physically guide the child's hand with a very light touch every now and then, to ensure success.

Step 3 - Child as overt commentator
Firstly the child is instructed to explain the task, "Tell me what it is that you are going to do?" "Now show me." Then they are encouraged to talk out loud explaining what they are doing, as they do the task.

Step 4 - Child as semi-overt commentator
Next stage is for the child to talk very quietly as they whisper the instructions to themselves. It may help to tell the child to tell themselves what it is that they are doing.

Step 5 - Child as covert commentator
Finally the child completes the task while providing their own inner speech to guide and control their behaviour.

To achieve success in this process takes time, but you are helping children acquire an essential skill for self-control.

As we can see there are many aspects to self-control. Some children will have weaknesses in a number of areas that need strengthening, while others will need to learn new ones. To develop an appropriate programme for a specific child we need to know:

1. the skills needed for self-control
2. methods to develop techniques to improve those skills

1. Key skills
1. Problem solving - the ability to recognise difficulties and to generate ideas to overcome obstacles.
2. Self-talk - children's ability to use language to understand, comment on and monitor their own behaviour.
3. Consequences - through experience children predict the different outcomes, positive and negative, of their behaviour.

4. Relaxation - because self-control, thinking, is extremely difficult when a child is emotionally aroused. This is the skill to control the negative effects of strong emotions.
5. Memory and time - it is essential that children have an understanding and ability to estimate periods of time. This is a must for the impulsive child.

Because we will be working with children of different ages and abilities we will need a wide range of techniques to enable appropriate programmes to be designed for any specific child. Below are a range of techniques that have been effectively used to develop the skills we are focusing on.

2. Techniques

Modelling - a range of techniques which involve children observing either an adult, child, or cartoon character display certain skills in a situation that is personally relevant for the child, for example as in social stories.

Self-awareness - a child is helped to understand the role of thinking in deciding what to do as well as the need to use "inner speech" to check things out.

Fantasy - children using internal images, sounds and smells which enable them to imagine, rehearse and learn from real or imagined events.

Behaviours - skills that children can practise and which can be observed by them and others.

Feelings - helping children to use the internal experiences which occur in reaction to both external/internal events which can be either pleasant or distressing.

Clearly depending on the age and ability of the children we are working with, some methods will be more appropriate than others. While most older children will be able to use fantasy, feelings and awareness, younger ones are less likely to.

To develop each of the five key skills we now have a choice of five different methods.

For each skill there are two techniques given as examples. This means that there will be ten techniques suggested for each skill to be developed, made up from the different methods. This is indicated in Figure 1 on the next page.

METHODS		Modelling	Self-Awareness	Fantasy	Behaviour	Feelings
S	**problem solving**	1/2	3/4	5/6	7/8	9/10
K	**self-talk**	1/2	3/4	5/6	7/8	9/10
I	**consequences**	1/2	3/4	5/6	7/8	9/10
L	**relaxation**	1/2	3/4	5/6	7/8	9/10
L	**time & memory**	1/2	3/4	5/6	7/8	9/10
S						

Figure 1

Each of the skills will now be presented with ten example techniques for each, two from each of the five methods.

Skill to be developed - Problem solving skills

Definitions
Problem solving is the ability to create rational solutions to the challenges children meet. It involves the skills of defining the problem and deciding which solution is the "best fit".

Modelling
1. Use videos, comics, stories to find examples of problem solving. Discuss with the child what is going on, consequences etc.
2. Design real problem situations and explain to the child how you would work out what you would do. Try concrete problems such as, "Tyre on bike keeps losing air" and social problems such as, "Pupil keeps shouting out answers instead of waiting."

Self-awareness
3. Teach the child a three-step problem solving model.
        STOP   THINK   CHOOSE

With examples work through a range of solutions, and through looking at consequences let the child practise the process.
4. With the child develop a range of self-talk skills.
   - "I can work this out."
   - "I'll go for a quick walk and then decide what to do."
   - "When I think negatively I'll pinch myself and then use my relaxation skills."

Fantasy
5. The child practises imagining a situation where they stayed in control and practised their skills. They are asked to picture the scene in minute detail. This would involve who is there, what are they wearing, are they inside a house or outside? etc.
6. The child rehearses a situation where they often lose control and rehearse in their mind what they could do, how different options would work out.

Behaviours
7. At the end of each day they fill in a Problem Solving account of situations where they felt they stayed in control.
8. The child practises a number of things to do whenever they get into situations in which they usually act impulsively, going to a quiet area, reading through a small "problem solving" reminder.

Feelings
9. The child learns key techniques which avoid immediate over-arousal. These include muscle relaxation through tensing and relaxing different muscle groups and breathing slowly and deeply, breathing in to the count of 7 and out to the count of 11.
10. The child has a number of "imaginary places" which they associate with being extremely calm and relaxed. They associate key words with such memories as well as certain actions, for example touching the tip of their thumb to their index finger.

Skill to be developed - Self-talk as control

Definitions
Self-talk is how we each control and monitor our behaviour internally. The newer the situation the more we may be aware of this internal speech, but much of the time it passes unnoticed.

Modelling

1. For young children use the Developing Inner Speech Control process as described above. But if there are phases that a child finds difficult, for example Phase 5, it would be unwise to persist. Choose those methods which naturally fit with a child's existing skills.

Phase 1   Child observes as adult does task with running commentary
Phase 2   Child does task with adult's parallel commentary
Phase 3   Child does task and provides overt commentary
Phase 4   Child does task with minimum vocal commentary
Phase 5   Child does task with covert "inner speech"

2. The focus child spends time with a pupil who has good self-control skills. At the end of a period a "debrief session" looks for skills used. Stage manage a "role-play" improvisation and ask the model pupil how they would react.

Self-awareness

3. The child monitors certain aspects of their behaviour and works to increase positive aspects.
4. A list of useful "inner speech" examples are produced for a child to carry and practise for themselves. Examples are:
What do I want to get out of this situation?
Have I got the skills to achieve this?
What do I need to be able to do?

Fantasy

5. The child creates an image that can be used to slow down impulsive tendencies. An image that contradicts speed will help. For example, the child reminds themselves that "I will go slow enough for Tommy the Tortoise to keep up with me." A toy tortoise may be helpful to give younger children a concrete object to remember.
6. A personalised rap or mnemonic can help older children remember how to talk to themselves positively. Sue Tickled Chris = Stop Think Choose.

Behaviour

7. With an adult, the child learns when they are impulsive. Is it work-related? Does it happen with friends? If there are particular circumstances can these situations be changed or avoided, or will the child need to plan an agreed set of actions?

8. The child agrees a specific reward after using Self-control techniques.

Feelings
9. The child is given a number of positive words to encourage feelings that will help them feel good:
CALM   POSITIVE   HAPPY.
10. The child has positive self-statements that they learn off by heart and repeat whenever negative feelings begin.
"Three things I am good at. Something I can do better now is…"

Skill to be developed - Understanding consequences

Definitions
Consequences refers to the outcomes that occur as a result of a child's behaviour. They can be either positive, negative or indifferent. A child is motivated to obtain those they enjoy and avoid those they find unpleasant.

Modelling
1. Using videos and stories the child is taught to focus and to learn to predict the consequences of certain behaviours and label the key emotion present.
2. With an adult, the child draws up a menu of consequences and divides them into those they like and those they don't. The positive ones are then ranked according to desirability.

Self-awareness
3. The child is given a range of "feeling" words and asked to match them to different situations. For example, anger or sadness at their bike being stolen, happiness and pleasure at winning a holiday and kindness and care at helping a friend out of a difficulty.
4. The child is helped to understand the internal cues that tell us how we are feeling. Reading emotions from facial expressions can also be used.

Fantasy
5. Using an imaginary person, create stories with a character acting impulsively in similar ways to the focus child. Agree consequences if the character can solve the problem. The child acts as director to ensure success.

6. Each day the child rehearses the strategies they will use in certain situations to obtain agreed consequences.

Behaviour
7. A range of positive consequences are agreed with the focus child working to achieve improvements such as increased work output in set lessons.
8. Parents/carers at home agree benefits with the child when set targets are achieved. These could include trips, presents, activities etc.

Feelings
9. The child explores the outcomes of a range of positive and negative situations.
10. The child is given a number of ways of reacting when faced with problem situations, eg key people to look for, key peers who will offer support, permission to "have time out'.

Skill to be developed - Relaxation

Definitions
Relaxation is the process through which understanding specific techniques can be used to prevent negative emotions blocking positive thoughts, actions and feelings.

Modelling
1. Through role play the child is shown the different facial expressions and body postures associated with different feelings.
2. The child observes popular TV programmes which show how different people react to different stressors.

Self-awareness
3. The child is taught the different ways in which stress can affect how we think, feel and act. They then work out their own "stress print" which shows how they respond to stress.
4. Using age-appropriate diagrams the child is shown how the brain and body respond to outside threats, fight or flight.

Fantasy
5. Using guided imagery the child looks at situations that they found difficult but coped with. The adult teases out the child's coping strategies.

6. The child is helped to create a guided fantasy journey that contains a range of events, activities, sights and sounds that they find relaxing.

Behaviour
7. The child works out a daily exercise programme, such as sport, walking, swimming and breathing exercises.
8. The child practises "acting as if" they have certain qualities they would like to have. How would they stand and walk and talk if they were brave, kind, determined, positive, purposeful, etc.

Feelings
9. The child is helped to generate a list of feeling words and to link them to different situations that typically give rise to them. They then look at healthy emotional reactions, for example anger at losing a team game, and unhealthy ones such as feeling guilty that they have hurt someone unintentionally.
10. The child is helped to work out an "ideal" programme that would enable them to experience as many positive emotions each day as possible. What would they do to feel - happy, positive, kind, determined, loyal, trustworthy, dependable and brave?

Skill to be developed - Time and memory

Definitions
Time and memory involves a child being able to relate actions to the passing of time. With impulsive children it is essential that they are aware of the need for time to pass to enable certain actions or processes to be undertaken. To think through a plan of action cannot be done in three seconds.

Modelling
1. Through role play the child is shown the different ways in which the passing of time can be estimated. Short periods - One banana, two bananas; longer periods - doing certain tasks to fill time.
2. The child is encouraged to make lists of the different things they have to do as a way of not forgetting.

Self-awareness
3. The child is taught the different ways of measuring the passing of time, clocks with second hands, egg-timers, sundials, candles, etc.

4. Using specific examples the child is shown how they have a short-term and a long-term memory. The short-term will forget things because it is limited - which is why we need ideas to help us remember.

Fantasy
5. Using guided imagery the child imagines doing various activities and estimates how long they would take. The adult develops a measurement for the child to relate to activities they know of. For example:

3 SECS	=	the time it takes to breathe in and out
10 MINS	=	time taken to walk home
30 MINS	=	the length of a favourite TV programme
2 HRS	=	length of a favourite video
1 DAY	=	how long it takes to drive to grandparents

6. The child is helped to create a guided fantasy journey that contains a whole range of exciting objects and events and then has to remember as many as possible. The child could leave objects that belonged to them to enhance them remembering where they had left them.

Behaviour
7. The child is helped to estimate how long it might take to do a set task and then uses egg timers to see how close they were.
8. The child plays "Kim's Game" where some 20 objects are shown to them and then they are covered and one removed, or they have to remember as many as they can. The adult gives the child ideas for associating the objects together, for example the BUTTON was looking for the PENCIL.

Feelings
9. The child is helped to learn a list of time words and to link them to different emotional memories and needs that match them. For example:

45 SEC	=	Time taken to suck a sweet	FUN
2/3 MINS	=	Time taken for can of drink	THIRSTY
5 MINS	=	Time for average chocolate bar	HUNGRY
7 MINS	=	Time for 1 ice-cream	DELICIOUS
10 - 15 MIN	=	Meal in school	RUSHING

(Think of the fun in working out such a scale!)

10. The child is helped to work out ways of passing time when they are in a "hurry". What games could they play in their head to pass time and not just feel bored and frustrated? Such games could include:

Find five things that begin with the letters of my first name.
Five animals beginning with D, then plants, countries etc.

It is important to remember that very few of the above techniques are suitable for all children. Some assume a level of understanding that your child does not yet have. You may find though that the idea may prompt another that is just right. You should not use those that you are not happy with or do not feel will be right for the child you have in mind. Often it "ain't what you do, but the way that you do it," which brings success.

You will by now feel more informed and confident about supporting children who lack "self-control", and the next time someone describes a child as "being impulsive", you will be able to say, "I have a few ideas that just might help!"

The record sheet that follows is an example of some of the questions that you will need to answer when working to develop "self-control". Although some of the questions will not apply to the child you are working with, they will help you to focus in specifically as to which skills you are trying to develop.

The Record of Self-Control:
a skills approach

Child's Name ....

Adult Supporter ....

Date ....

---

1. Discuss and agree a goal with child.

---

2. Do you need to teach the child "inner speech" to help control and monitor their behaviour? How will you achieve this?

3. Do you need to develop the child's visual memory to rehearse new skills? How will you do this?

4. How will the child be rewarded for progress?

5. How will the child relax to enable them to control their emotional arousal when practising new self-control skills?

6. How will you develop the child's ability to remember different periods of time?

References

Brigham, T. (1989) *Self-Management for Adolescents,* The Guilford Press: New York.

Howe, M. (1988) *Treating Problem Children: Issues, Methods & Practice,* Sage Publications: London.

O'Rourke, K. & Worzbyt, J. (1996) *Support Groups for Children,* Accelerated Development: Washington.

Strayhorn, J. (1988) *The Competent Child,* The Guilford Press: New York.